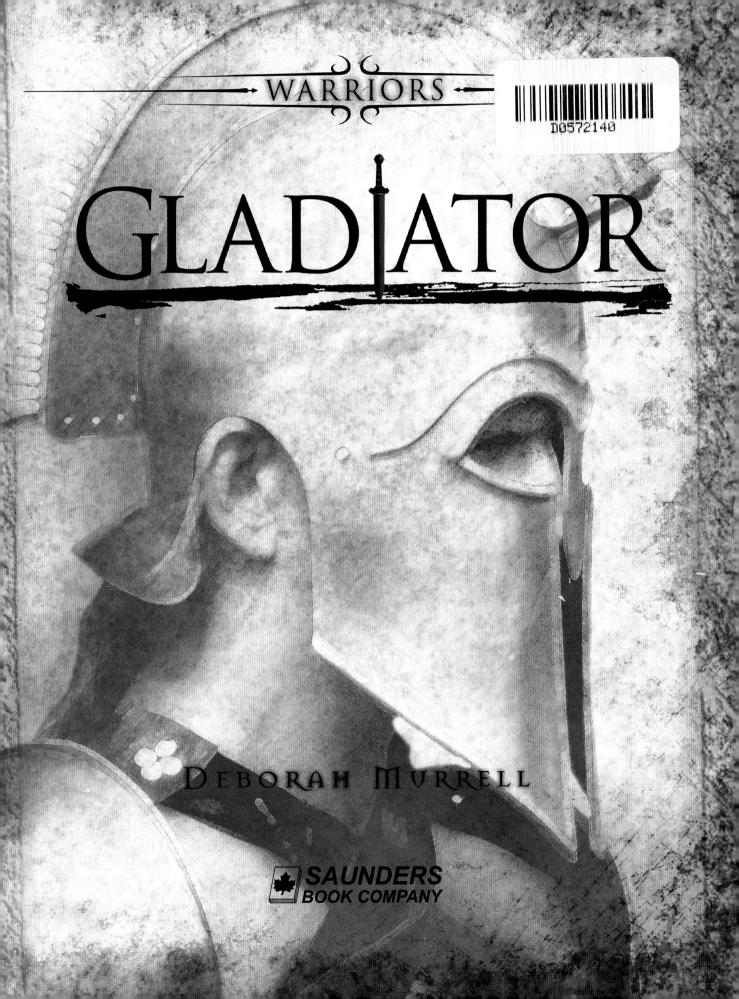

WARRIORS

GLADIATOR

DEBORAH MURRELL

SAUNDERS
BOOK COMPANY

Copyright © QEB Publishing, Inc. 2009

Published in 2011 by
Saunders Book Company
27 Stewart Road
Collingwood, ON Canada L9Y 4M7

www.qed-publishing.co.uk

All rights reserved. No part of this publication may be reproduced, stored in a retrieval system, or transmitted in any form or by any means, electronic, mechanical, photocopying, recording, or otherwise, without the prior permission of the publisher, nor be otherwise circulated in any form of binding or cover other than that in which it is published and without a similar condition being imposed on the subsequent purchaser.

Library of Congress Cataloging-in-Publication Data
Murrell, Deborah Jane, 1963-
  Gladiator / written by Deborah Murrell.
    p. cm. -- (QEB warriors)
  Includes index.
  ISBN 978-1-926853-52-9 (paperback)
  1. Gladiators--Juvenile literature. I. Title.
  GV35.M87 2010
  796.8'0937--dc22
                                    2009003540

Author Deborah Murrell
Consultant Philip Steele
Project Editor Eve Marleau
Designer and
  Picture Researcher Andrew McGovern
Illustrator Peter Dennis

Printed in China

Picture credits

Key: t=top, b=bottom, r=right, l=left, c=center
Alamy 6r The Print Collector, 9b Photo12, 15b PhotoBliss, 25t Photo12
Bridgeman 5b, 7b, 19r, 22–23, 24 Roger Payne, 25t Photo12, 25b Giorgio de Chirico
Corbis 2l Bettmann, 18–19 Bettmann, 29t Roger Wood
DK Images 16–17, 17b
Photolibrary 20–21, 26–27, 28–29 Bill Bachmann
Scala 5t Hermann Buresch, 21b Photo Scala, Florence – courtesy of the Ministero Beni e Att Culturali
Topfoto 13l Topham Picturepoint, 25b Roger-Viollet

The words in **bold** are explained in the Glossary on page 30.

CONTENTS

WHAT WAS A GLADIATOR?

A gladiator was a professional fighter in Roman times. Gladiator fights took place in large, round buildings called amphitheaters, often in front of thousands of people.

Gladius

The word "gladiator" comes from the Latin word *gladius*. This is the name for the short sword used by many gladiators. The sword was also used by soldiers in the Roman army.

➤ *Gladiators fought in the center of the amphitheater, on a floor covered with sand.*

➤ *Most gladiators were trained in a* **ludus**, *or school.*

Who were gladiators?

Gladiators were mainly men who were slaves, criminals, or prisoners of war. They were kept locked up, and forced to fight. If a gladiator was very good, and won many fights, he might be freed and, sometimes, earn money.

Female gladiators

A few women fought as gladiators. Most Romans did not approve of women in the **arena**, so they were not often seen there. **Emperor** Nero enjoyed watching female gladiators. He even made some noble women fight each other.

➤*Emperor Nero was a supporter of the gladiator games.*

WHEN DID GLADIATORS LIVE?

The first recorded gladiator fight among Romans took place in ancient Rome in 264 BC, in the *Forum Boarium*, or cattle market. It was part of the funeral for an important Roman citizen.

Emperor Augustus ruled from 27 BC to AD 14.

Ancient Rome

Rome was originally ruled by kings who were advised by **senators**. The last king, Tarquinius, was removed in 510 BC. Senators then ruled Rome as a **republic**, and tried to conquer the land around it. Army generals became very powerful. In 49 BC, the general Julius Caesar took control, but he was murdered soon afterward. In 27 BC his adopted son, Octavian, or Augustus, became the first emperor.

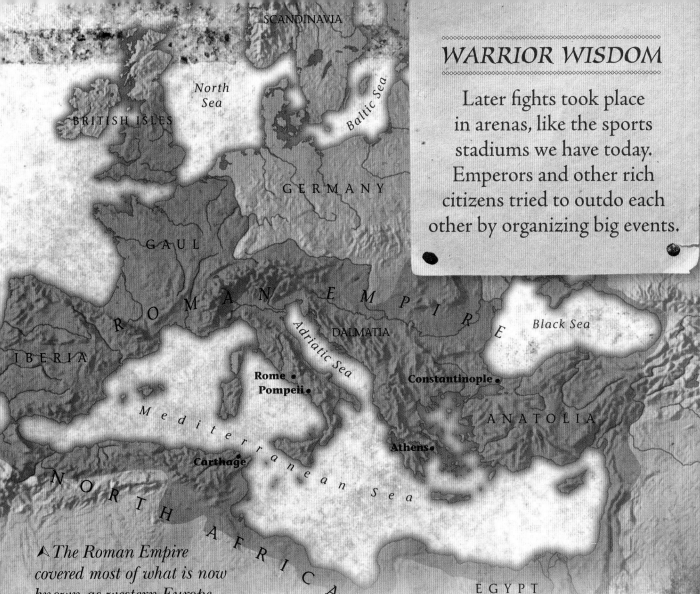

SCANDINAVIA

North
Sea

BRITISH ISLES

Baltic Sea

GERMANY

GAUL

R O M A N   E M P I R E

Adriatic Sea

DALMATIA

Black Sea

IBERIA

Rome •
Pompeii •

Constantinople •

A N A T O L I A

M e d i t e r r a n e a n   S e a

Athens •

Carthage •

N O R T H   A F R I C A

E G Y P T

↟ *The Roman Empire covered most of what is now known as western Europe.*

WARRIOR WISDOM

Later fights took place in arenas, like the sports stadiums we have today. Emperors and other rich citizens tried to outdo each other by organizing big events.

THE FIRST FIGHTERS

The Romans weren't the only ancient people to enjoy bloody fights and other gory shows. In fact, they may have got the idea from the Etruscans or the Campanians—two peoples in Italy who enjoyed watching men fight.

GLADIATOR SCHOOL

Gladiators needed to put on a good show for the audience. They had to go to a special school, called a *ludus*. Many of the teachers had been successful gladiators themselves.

Ludus

When a man joined a *ludus* at the age of about 17, he swore an oath, or promise. In this oath he agreed to being burned, chained, and beaten by his teachers when training, and to being killed in the ring. Most gladiators lived at the school, and were guarded so that they could not escape.

Training

Gladiators trained using wooden weapons. They practiced by attacking a wooden post stuck in the ground, or sometimes a sack filled with straw. Gladiators lived together and trained together in the *ludus*. Many of them became friends.

◄ *The* ludus *had a small arena where gladiators practiced their fighting skills.*

GLADIATOR

The film *Gladiator* (2000) is about a fictional general called Maximus Decimus Meridius. He refuses to serve the emperor's son, who has killed his own father to control the empire. Maximus is sold into a *ludus*.

RETIARII, MYRMILLONES, AND SAMNES

Different types of gladiator used various kinds of weapon and armor. Gladiators such as *retiarii*, *myrmillones*, and *samnes* didn't wear much armor at all.

Retiarii

The name *retiarii* means "net men" in Latin. These gladiators fought with a net and a **spear** with three tips, called a **trident**. They only wore armor on their left arm and shoulder, and tried to capture their enemy in the net before they attacked them.

WARRIOR WISDOM

Retiarii were trained to fight gladiators called *secutores* ("chasers"). These gladiators wore helmets with very small eye holes to stop *retiarii* stabbing them in the face with their tridents.

▲Retiarii *tried to capture their enemy by throwing a net over them.*

Myrmillones

These gladiators wore helmets with a large, finlike **crest**. They carried a sword and a large shield. *Myrmillones'* arms and legs were wrapped in fabric. *Myrmillones* never fought each other.

△ *The crests of myrmillones' helmets were made of horse hair.*

Samnes

Samnes gladiators were named after a group of tribes who fought many battles against Rome. They wore a helmet, armor on their sword arm, and a **greave** on one leg.

➤ Samnes *carried a short sword and rectangular shield.*

PROVOCATORES, EQUITES, AND VELITES

Some kinds of gladiator, such as *provocatores*, *equites*, and *velites*, only ever fought gladiators of the same type as themselves. As long as they were as fit and strong as each other, the fight would be a fair one.

Provocatores

These "challengers" wore a helmet with a **visor**, a piece of armor called a breastplate, and a greave on one leg. They also had armor on their sword arm, and carried a large shield.

➤ Provocatores *wore breastplates. Gladiators who fought without them were thought to be much braver.*

Equites

These gladiators fought on horseback.
Their name, *equites*, means "horsemen" in
Latin. *Equites* wore a helmet and a tunic,
and wrapped their legs and sword arm in
fabric. They also carried a round shield.
Equites only fought other *equites*.

Velites

Velites had a special
spear that was attached
to a long strap. It could
be pulled back so the
gladiator could throw the
spear again and again.
The Latin name for this
kind of spear was
hasta amentata.
Amentare meant "to
throw something
using a strap".

◄ *Equites used a long lance
and a sword in a fight.*

◄ *Some soldiers were called
velites in the Roman army.
These gladiators were
named after them.*

WARRIOR WISDOM

Gladiators were fed plenty
of food, including beans and
barley, so that they had the
energy to train and become
strong. For this reason, they
were often referred to as
hordearii, or "barley men".

GLADIATORS OF THE EMPIRE

The griffin on thraeces' helmets had an eagle's head and a lion's body.

Many emperors used the games as a way of showing how powerful they were in comparison to tribes they had conquered. They also helped the tribes feel they were part of the empire, protected by the strength of Rome. As the empire grew, gladiator fighting spread far and wide.

Thraeces

These gladiators (named after the Thracian tribe) wore protection on their sword arms. **Thraeces** had small, rectangular shields, and used curved swords. Their helmets were decorated with a griffin—a creature that the Romans believed guarded the dead.

Hoplomachi

The armor of **hoplomachi** was similar to *thraeces'* armor. Unlike the *thraeces, hoplomachi* used a rectangular shield and fought with a spear and sword. They threw the spear at their enemy early on in the fight, and then fought the rest of the battle with the sword. *Hoplomachi* looked like one of Rome's old enemies, the Greek hoplite soldiers. This is where the name *hoplomachi* comes from.

◄Hoplomachi *had very similar helmets to* thraeces.

EMPERORS IN THE RING

Some emperors even fought as gladiators themselves. Emperor Commodus (AD 161–192) claimed to have fought hundreds of times without getting hurt—no one dared harm the emperor!

THE COLOSSEUM

In AD 80, a new amphitheater was opened to the public in Rome. It was a large, circular building with seats around the outside and a large space in the middle for entertainment. It was later to be known as the Colosseum.

Seating

Let the games begin

The Colosseum was meant to please the public. To celebrate its opening, gladiator games went on for 100 days. The Colosseum could seat up to 50,000 people and towered over the city of Rome, at more than 187 feet (57 meters) in height.

Corridor

◄ *The audience in the Colosseum watched the games from many tiers, or levels, of seating.*

Awning

Arena

Sea battles

Many people believe that Emperor Titus had the Colosseum's arena flooded with water, so that a "sea" battle could be staged, with gladiators fighting on board ships.

▲ *If a sea battle, or* naumachia, *took place at the Colosseum, it would have been small. Larger battles were staged outside Rome in river basins.*

THE BUILD-UP

Most gladiator games were held on public holidays. Advertisements for the games, with lists of the fighters, were painted on the city walls. Some people bet money on which gladiator they thought would win.

On parade

Gladiators were owned by rich men. Many of these men brought them to town especially for the games. They walked through the streets while someone called out their names and skills. This was so people could decide who they thought was a winner.

Souvenirs

People set up **souvenir** stalls around the town and sold objects to remind people of the games. All of these were decorated with images of something to do with the games, such as weapons or gladiators fighting each other.

◄ *Romans made bets on which gladiator they thought would win, depending on how strong they looked in the parade.*

➤ *Clay figures, oil-lamps, and knives were sold on souvenir stalls.*

WARRIOR WISDOM

As the Roman Empire grew and became richer, there were more and more public holidays—at one point, they had 159 days a year! Of these, 93 were used for gladiator games.

THE AUDIENCE

Tickets for the games were given to people of the highest classes, and passed on to friends and supporters. They then passed them on to their friends, and so on, down to the lower classes.

▼ *The audience watches as gladiators salute the emperor Julius Caesar before the fights begin.*

The best seats in the house

Depending on their place in society, different people were allowed into different areas of the Colosseum. Closest to the ring were the very rich and important men. The emperor, of course, had the best seat in the house—right at the front.

The general public

Women and girls sat in the highest seats, furthest from the stage. These were the worst seats in the house for watching the action. Below the women were slaves and poor people, then soldiers and ordinary citizens.

RIOT!

Public games were very noisy and busy. A fresco, or wall painting, at Pompeii shows a riot in the crowd that took place in AD 59. Many people were killed or wounded. Gladiator shows were banned in Pompeii for years afterward.

THE BIG DAY

There were many different kinds of event to entertain the audience on the day of the games. The show usually started with animal hunts and criminal executions. It was not until the afternoon that the gladiators began to fight.

Animal hunts

In the morning, creatures such as bulls and elephants were released into the ring to fight each other. Sometimes they were hunted by men armed with spears. Exotic animals from around the empire were shown to the audience to remind them how much of the world was ruled by the Romans.

⌃ Sometimes the animals were so scared that they had to be chased by other men to make them fight the gladiators.

Emperor Augustus
(63 BC–AD 14) boasted that
in the 26 wild animal hunts
he put on, 3,500 creatures
were killed. In the opening
games at the Colosseum,
Emperor Titus (AD 39–81)
had 9,000 animals killed.

The warm-up

The afternoon's entertainment often began
with comedy fights. Next, there was a
parade of men carrying the weapons and
armor for the gladiators. The gladiators
then had a warm-up fight. When the
trumpets sounded, it was time for the
gladiators to get ready for the main event.

FIGHT!

Gladiators normally fought one-on-one. The two men were equally matched in strength so the fight would not end too quickly.

▼ *Each gladiator was fighting for his life. If he fought well, he might be spared.*

Showdown

A typical afternoon at the gladiator games involved around ten to 12 fights. Fights might be anywhere from two to 15 minutes long. Some fights lasted so long that both gladiators were too exhausted to go on. In these cases, they were allowed to live.

SPARTACUS

Spartacus was a gladiator who led a revolt against the Romans in 73 BC. He escaped from his *ludus* with other men, but they were defeated in 71 BC by the Roman army. Stanley Kubrick made a film in 1960 about the life of Spartacus, starring Kirk Douglas.

Going back in time

Sometimes gladiators were made to **re-enact** famous battles. In 46 BC, Julius Caesar ordered a huge battle. Each army had 500 foot soldiers, 20 elephants and 30 gladiators on horseback.

▼Reenactments of famous battles could involve many gladiators at a time.

WIN OR LOSE

Gladiators usually fought until it was clear that one of them was going to win. A gladiator always tried to impress the audience with his skill so that, even if he lost, the audience might encourage the emperor to let him live.

Decision time

If the emperor decided that the loser should die, the winning gladiator had to cut the loser's throat. The winner tried to make the death a quick one. The loser might have been a friend from his *ludus*.

➤ *The winning gladiator looked to the emperor to see whether he should kill his opponent or let him live.*

Thumbs up or thumbs down

It was the right of the emperor, or the person who had paid for the games, to decide whether a loser would live or die. The public used their thumbs to show whether they wanted the loser to live or not—but it is not known which way the audience held their thumbs when they did this.

WARRIOR WISDOM

If a gladiator died in the fight, the audience wanted to make sure that he was dead. The gladiator was poked with a hot iron to see if he reacted. After he had been taken out of the ring, his throat would be cut, just to be on the safe side!

THE END OF GLADIATORS

By the AD 400s, the Roman Empire had become weaker. It was attacked by many enemies, and its leaders often fought for power among themselves.

End of the show

Emperor Constantine banned the games in AD 326. Other emperors tried to start them up again, but they never became as popular as they once had been. In AD 400, Emperor Honorius banned them forever.

PIN-UPS

Gladiators were very famous in ancient Rome, just like today's sports stars. Many mosaics have been found of all the different types of gladiator.

▼ *Thousands of tourists visit the Colosseum ruins every year.*

Ruins

After the gladiator games ended, the Colosseum was no longer used. People took stones from it to use in new buildings. Today, it is one of Rome's main tourist attractions.

GLOSSARY

Amphitheater A round or oval building with seating around a central arena for sporting or entertainment events.

Arena A level area surrounded by seating, in which public events are held.

Armor Protective clothing, often made of metal or leather.

Citizen A free man in Roman society.

Class A person's position in the community.

Crest A ridge or plume sticking up from the top of a helmet.

Emperor The ruler of an empire.

Empire A large number of states ruled over by a person, a group of people or another state.

Equites Gladiators who fought on horseback.

Fresco A painting made on wet plaster.

Funeral A ceremony in which a dead person is buried or cremated.

Greave Armour worn on the legs.

Hoplomachi Gladiators who fought with a sword and spear.

Ludus A kind of school in which gladiators were trained to fight.

Myrmillones Gladiators who fought with a sword and shield. They wore a crested helmet.

Provocatores Gladiators who fought with a sword and shield, and wore a helmet with a visor.

Re-enact To act out past events.

Republic A country or state ruled by a group of people.

Retiarii Gladiators who fought with a net and trident.

Samnes Gladiators who fought with a short sword and rectangular shield.

Senator A member of the council that ruled ancient Rome.

Souvenir An object made to remind someone of a particular day or event.

Spear A long pole with a sharp tip, used for throwing or stabbing.

Thraeces Gladiators who fought with a small, curved sword and small shield.

Trident A kind of three-pronged spear.

Velites Gladiators who fought with a spear attached to a long strap.

Visor Part of a helmet that can be pulled down to protect the face.

INDEX

Crowsnest Pass Municipal Library

DEC 2 0 2010